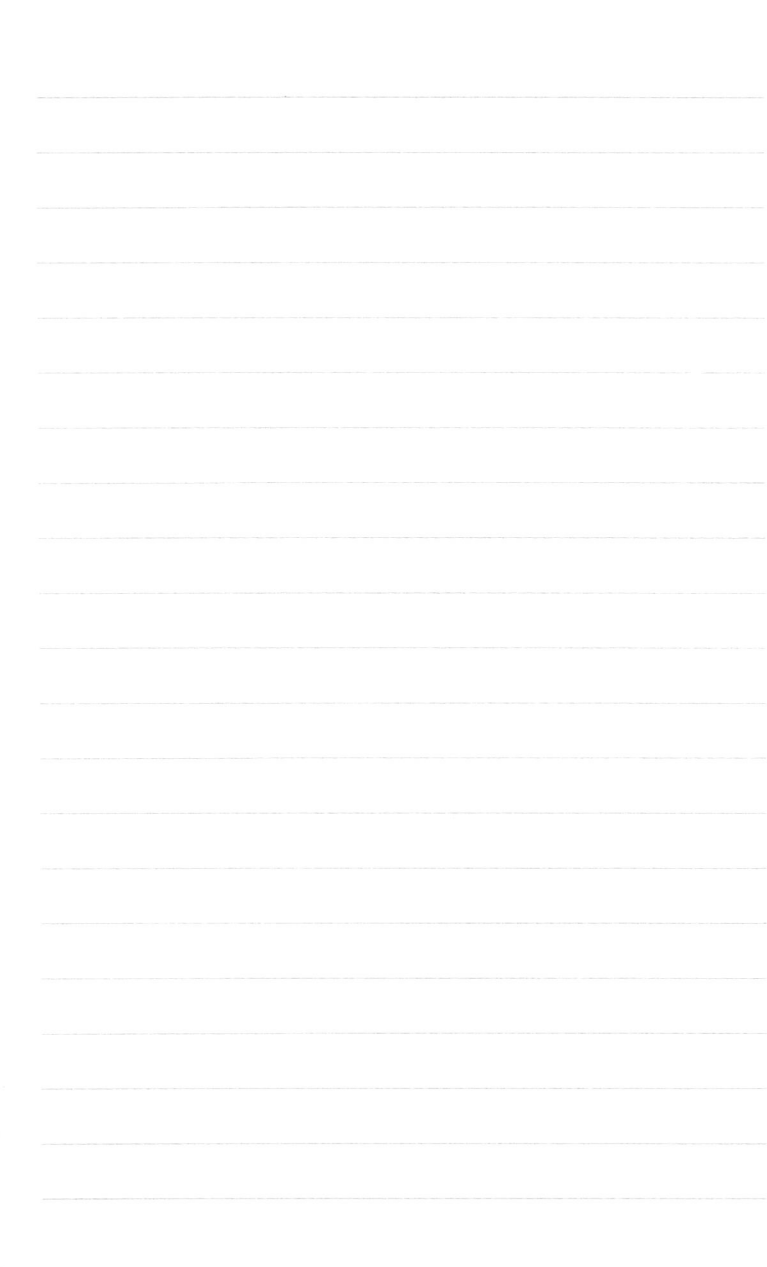

paperblanks®
SACRED TIBETAN
TEXTILES

Les traditions artistiques, religieuses et culturelles s'unissent sur les tissus représentés sur nos carnets Textiles Tibétains Sacrés. Pendant des siècles, les familles musulmanes de Varanasi (Inde) ont pratiqué l'art du tissage pour confectionner des vêtements de cérémonie pour les rituels. Les tissus reproduits sur nos carnets proviennent directement du magasin de la famille Kasim et retranscrivent l'authenticité de leur héritage culturel. Sur ce tissu crée pour un monastère bouddhiste, les tisserands ont voulu représenter le chemin de l'illumination, à la fois grâce au motif symbolique et à la clarté des couleurs.

Künstlerische, religiöse und kulturelle Traditionen vereinen sich in unserem Muster Heilige tibetische Stoffe. Seit Jahrhunderten widmen sich mohammedanische Familien in Varanasi, Indien, der Seidenweberei per Hand zur Herstellung von Stoffen für heilige Rituale. Der auf unserem Einband reproduzierte Stoff kommt direkt aus dem Warenhaus der Familie Kasim und ist der wahre Ausdruck ihres kulturellen Erbes. In diesem Muster, das für ein buddhistisches Kloster bestimmt ist, wird der Weg zur Erleuchtung gezeigt, sowohl mittels der symbolischen Formen als auch durch die gewählten leuchtenden Farben.

Le tradizioni artistiche, religiose e culturali si uniscono nel tessuto intrecciato a mano del disegno dei Tessuti Sacri Tibetani. Per secoli le famiglie musulmane di Varanasi, in India, hanno praticato l'arte della tessitura a mano della seta per creare panni e vestiti per rituali sacri. Il tessuto riprodotto sulle nostre copertine arriva direttamente dall'emporio di seta di Kasim ed è un'espressione autentica del patrimonio culturale dei tessitori. In questo disegno, creato per un monastero buddista, i tessitori hanno rappresentato il percorso dell'illuminazione, sia tramite il motivo simbolico che con la luminosità dei colori scelti.

Tradiciones artísticas, religiosas y culturales confluyen en la tela artesanal de este diseño de nuestra colección Tejidos Tibetanos Sagrados. Durante siglos, las familias musulmanas de Varanasi (India) han practicado el arte del tejido de la seda para confeccionar textiles y vestimentas para rituales sagrados. El tejido que reproducimos en esta cubierta procede de Kasim Silk Emporium, en Varanasi, y es expresión auténtica de la herencia cultural del tejedor. En este diseño, creado para un monasterio budista, el tejedor ha reflejado el camino hacia la iluminación, tanto en el motivo simbólico como en el brillo de los colores elegidos.

手織りの布のなかで、芸術、宗教、文化の伝統が1つに融合されています。インドのバラナシに暮らすイスラム教徒たちは、数世紀にわたって、手織りの絹地を使い神聖な儀式のための布や祭服を作ってきました。このデザインはバラナシにある織物会社Kasim Silk Emporiumで作られた布を再現したものであり、同社の持つ伝統を忠実に表現しています。もともとは仏教寺院のために織られたものであり、象徴的な文様と明るい色彩によって、悟りに至るまでの道が描かれています。

paperblanks®
SACRED TIBETAN TEXTILES

Ashta

Artistic, religious and cultural traditions unite in the handwoven fabric of this Sacred Tibetan Textiles design. For centuries, Muslim families in Varanasi, India, have practiced the art of handweaving silks to create cloths and vestments for sacred rituals. The fabric reproduced on this cover comes straight from the Kasim Silk Emporium in Varanasi and is an authentic expression of the weaver's cultural heritage. In this design, created for a Buddhist monastery, the weavers have portrayed the path to enlightenment, both in the symbolic pattern and in the brightness of the colours chosen.

With this Sacred Tibetan Textiles journal, we pay tribute to the rich heritage of Indian handweaving and to the craftspeople who continue this devotional practice today.

ISBN: 978-1-4397-9353-4
MIDI FORMAT   176 PAGES   LINED
DESIGNED IN CANADA